Even That Indigo

John Smith

Hip Pocket Press Mission Statement

It is our belief that the arts are the embodiment of the soul of a culture, that the promotion of writers and artists is essential if our current culture, with its emphasis on television and provocative outcomes, is to have a chance to develop that inner voice and ear that express and listen to beauty. Toward that end, Hip Pocket Press will continue to search out and discover poets and writers whose voices can give us a clearer understanding of ourselves and of the culture which defines us.

Other Books from Hip Pocket Press

You Notice the Body: Gail Rudd Entrekin (poetry)
Terrain: Dan Bellm, Molly Fisk & Forrest Hamer (poetry)
A Common Ancestor: Marilee Richards (poetry)
Sierra Songs & Descants: Poetry & Prose of the Sierra
Truth Be Told: Tom Farber (epigrams)
Songs for a Teenage Nomad: Kim Culbertson (young adult fiction)
Yuba Flows: Kirsten Casey, Gary Cooke, Cheryl Dumesnil, Judy
      Halebsky, Iven Lourie & Scott Young (poetry)
The More Difficult Beauty: Molly Fisk (poetry)
*Ex Vivo (Out of the Living Body)*L Kirsten Casey (poetry)

Web Publications

Canary, a Literary Journal of the Environmental Crisis:
      www.hippocketpress.org/canary
Sisyphus, Essays on Language, Culture & the Arts:
      www.hippocketpress.org/sisyphus

Even That Indigo

John Smith

HPP
HIP POCKET PRESS

Orinda, CA
2012

Published by Hip Pocket Press
5 Del Mar Court
Orinda, CA 94563
www.hippocketpress.org

This edition was produced for on-demand distribution by
lightningsource.com for Hip Pocket Press.

Typesetting: Wordsworth (wordsworthofmarin.com)
Cover art: "Night Swimmers" (detail) 1997 by Michael McFadden
Cover design: Ron Lent
Photograph of author: Ron Lent

Printed in the United States of America.

ISBN: 0-917658-38-8
978-0-917658-38-9

For Catherine, Lauren, Tara, & Stella

ACKNOWLEDGMENTS

Some of these poems have been published in the following magazines:

Berkeley Poets Cooperative
Canary
Confluence
Delaware Valley Poets
Edison Literary Review
Exit 13
Journal of New Jersey Poets
The Literary Review
New Jersey Audubon
New York Quarterly
Northeast Corridor
Paterson Literary Review
Ragazine
Shot Glass Journal
Slant
US 1

I am grateful for my mother, who gave me the ocean; my father, who grew lunaria and taught me to peel back the skin of the moon; my sisters and brother, who have been with me all along; and my wife and daughters for the gift of themselves. I would also like to thank the following friends for helping make this book happen: Nancy Bennett, Pete Dunne, Gail Entrekin, Ross Gay, Lois Marie Harrod, Ron Lent, Michael McFadden, and Karen Malzone.

Contents

Even That Indigo   11

Red Moon   12

Oberly Road   13

United Ring and Seal   16

Pictures of a Fireman   18

Birding   20

One More Day   21

Orchid   22

Sea Glass   24

Swing Set   26

Stoop Ball   28

Stumbling Around in the Light   30

Poe Bernadette   32

What I Wanted of Milkweed   34

Seaside Heights   36

Timepiece   37

Peony   38

The Neighbor's Dog   39

Judas   40

The Only Symphony   42

The Original Tree   43

The Way of the Cage   44

Alpha   46

The Book   48

What Are the Odds of Moonlight?   50

Autumn Song   51

Winter Birds   52

Bright Green Hose, Early Sixties   53

Local Holy Wars   54

We Now Know   55

Lived Like a Saint   56

in the flock of geese   57

The Rabbit   58

Echo Lake   60

Dylan's Pool Cue   62

The Calling   63

Lilacs   64

Towpath   65

Bird Call   66

Snow Goose   68

What One of My Thoughts Thought When It Thought I Wasn't
     Paying Attention   70

Turning Over the Earth   72

I Didn't Go   74

Dreaming in Pompeii   75

A Case of Unopened Boxes   76

Tiny Moon   77

Way-back Seat   78

My Grandfather's Game   80

The Rewarded 82

this poem is called without frames 83

Into the Glare 84

Bonfire 86

Market Street 87

Primal Urge 88

Tending the Garden 89

The Great Swamp 90

Shroud of Frenchtown 91

Retired Anarchist 92

Cicada 93

I Got As Far As the Sycamore 94

Into Sycamore 95

Show of Teeth 96

Remnants 98

Reservoir 99

The Gourd's Complaint 100

Babble 101

Shrew 102

My Scribe 103

Birder's Last Blessing 104

Even That Indigo

The last blue through
my kitchen window
is indigo. Before a crow
swallows the sapphire
in the sky's dark bowl
and everything goes black,
it goes indigo, gets an
ultramarine sheen to it,
a nebulous blue and black stain,
like a painting by Rothko
or a trombone and cello duet
that makes the wild iris moan
deep in its throat, moan
like a pilot light
inside a dark stove.
The same indigo in the eye
of a cormorant
nodding on a snowbank in Antarctica
glows in the feathers of a bunting
calling from the forest edge
of my back yard.
You know the indigo,
like a blueberry, solo
in an ebony bowl,
before the kitchen goes black
and night takes back
even that indigo.

Red Moon

for Stella

When we meet at the river under a red moon,
together again, you an elderly woman, and I
long since dead, we will dance on the green bridge
above dark water like we did when you were the child
I shook from bed and bundled, the child who said,
*The moon must be going out tonight; she's putting on
her red dress*, as the white sphere slipped into
Earth's umbra. When we meet at the river, snow
on both shores, my forest and your city aglow,
what passes through floor-lit trees or neon streets
will not matter anymore. When we meet under
a red moon again, as it says in the old text,
The sky will roll up its scroll and stars fall like figs.
Dress, then, like the moon, my dear, wear red,
and we will dance in the fiery eclipse on a green bridge
between separate shores for the last time once more.

Winter Solstice 2010

Oberly Road

A white hill rose south of Oberly Road
like a small moon with one spindly tree
on top and a Rough-legged Hawk, descended
from Arctic tundra to winter on ample mice
and voles in the Alpha Grasslands,
perched like the last leaf in its crown.

***

Among a host of Savannah Sparrows,
a Snow Bunting pecked seed in the street.
I stopped, quietly focused, then vanished
between feather and wing.

***

Blanched, brittle corn stalks pierced
the snow. Quick-stepping in and out
of their broken maze, black-masked
Horned Larks tweaked dried kernels
from rusty cobs with stout beaks.
The exaltation bustled bare pock to pock,
spooked, surfed the frigid air singing,
su-weet, sweet, sweet, su-weet.

***

I remember when nothing was protected.
Farmer'd come running from his house,
chase cars halfway down the street
cursing birders cruising his roadside fields
for hawks and owls, larks, longspurs, and buntings.
Now the setting sun glares at the grasslands
from tall windows to the east,
and a bulldozer perched on the western ridge
like a hawk eyes the farmlands
as if the acres themselves were plump mice.

* * *

From his pickup truck, the farmer waved to me,
idling roadside with my binoculars,
as he passed by the small plot of preserved space.
I may have been just another birder
or he might have recognized my face,
or the same red Corolla over the years
has become part of the winter landscape to him,
a cardinal bigger than a cow. I bet he'd laugh at that.
I bet we weep about some of the same things.

* * *

Sweeping snowy corn rows
like bronze blades on a shaft of wind,
the harrier's feathered scythe
severed the last of the light.

* * *

It is almost too late to believe
that early in the twenty-first century
I witnessed fifty wild turkeys
flap, rustle, and clunk weary wings
against the frozen limbs
of a stand of quaking aspens along a creek.
They jockeyed for position
to safely roost a windy night in New Jersey,
their dark metronomes
keeping sleep.

***

That evening
the world was dreaming of snow
and sealed in a sheet of ice
polished with moonlight
so sturdy an old man could walk on it
like a child again.

United Ring and Seal

The summer before college
I worked United Ring and Seal
nine hours a day, six days a week
on my feet, fitting airplane
piston ring after airplane
piston ring into a rotor,
then lowering the lever
that lowered the blade that shaved
exactly however many millimeters
the military needed shaved
from the inside edge
to ensure smooth flying.

I sang every song I knew
and survived break to break
half grinding, half dancing,
caught up in the dull service
and rote worship
of some foreign purpose.

Punched in and out of time,
I skimmed by on cigarettes
outside on a bench leaning back
against the building,
the brick wall's thick hum
massaging my lucky shoulders,
sun resting its warm hand on my face.

And I thought about my friends
with lower lottery numbers than mine,
rifles raised over their wide-eyed heads,
mouths closed tight, glancing
side to side, advancing,
up to their armpits in Vietnam,
and I thought about the Vietnamese
leaning back like me
against machine shops
they didn't own either,
savoring their own small breaks,
while not only the walls behind them
but the clouds above were humming,
humming and dark with planes.

Pictures of a Fireman

Grandma said his eyes rose
like moons above the rim of his glasses
when he leaned over the table
at the pool hall the first time they met,
called every shot. I remember him
descending from a cloud
on a ladder of flames
with a woman in his arms,
clipped from the front page
of the *Newark Evening News*
and framed on their living room mantel.
Or as he was in the photograph I found
in an attic album of him tending register
behind the bar of a speakeasy,
his eyes dark, cheeks flushed,
grinning back at the camera
as if he owned the place.
I see him seaside, sometimes,
up to his knees in weekend surf,
his white, button-down shirt
flapped open like the wings
of a Great Egret, fishing pole bowed,
tip sparkling like a cufflink on a cloud
as he tugs at the ocean, hair black
and slicked back, as it always was,
even at his wake. I can't recall his voice
or a single thing he told me,
but I dangle on the soft lines of his face,
the dark-spotted skin, drawn thin
about his hands, how they would shake,

his cup and saucer rattle, steaming coffee
splash against the rim, and how his eyes
would rise above his glasses
like apologetic white flags,
then fall away from mine
as he leaned in cautiously for a sip.

Birding

Do you remember your first bird,
the way it scuttled across the lawn, stopped stiff,
tilted its head, and listened to the earth?
Don't you still need to hold still sometimes
and feel the world underfoot?
Aren't you plucked from this life
by such singing as unthreads each day,
struck by shadows soaring past your feet
and scaling the very buildings
that tower in your way?
Isn't a black silhouette perched in every tree?
Who among us hasn't sat up with the owls
interrogating the night?
Who hasn't been knocking on dead wood for years,
flapping through life, season by season,
squawking and warbling, warbling and squawking,
migrating, migrating, migrating?
Don't we all live on the wing,
teetering in the wind
from one nest to the next,
compelled by our own singing?

One More Day

I need one more day between Saturday and Sunday,
an extra twenty-four hours, wild and holy, with trains
and a stream running through it and bells from the other side
of the hill and a single plot, a modest garden, for lettuce,
cucumbers, and zucchini, and two kinds of peppers,
jalapeño and hot cherry. Just one more day for tomatoes
and basil, a couple of onions, a little olive oil, two or three,
maybe four cloves of garlic and enough salt to fill the spoon
of my palm. And basil: I can't forget basil. I need herbs:
Greek oregano and thyme. I need lots of thyme. I want to
keep bees like Virgil, feed them woolly and lemon thyme.
I want to stir a spoonful of thyme honey into my tea.
I would drink three cups a day. I need water and herbs.
And I need bread. Where would my tomato sauce be
without bread for the dipping? I'd have counter tops
and floor tiles dusted with flour, every crack in the oak table
puttied with dough, always a loaf rising in the oven.
I would keep two mugs—one for company—and one bowl.
If I invited someone to visit me, we would eat with our fingers
in front of the fireplace and talk with our hands.
But I could live alone forever for just one day a week.
In the woods with the wild flowers between an ash
and a tulip tree, I would hammock on moonlight
just this side or that of the katydids and the crickets.

Orchid

for Catherine

When I finally let my tongue
out of its cage,
the first thing it wanted to do
was fly back and forth
singing your name.
Because my right hand
is rooted five times in your soil,
you are always within reach.
And because our left hands
are tied ten times
to the sky,
we are bound together.
This isn't crazy.
Let's let what lies ahead
fall behind us
together,
nest in the air
and make love under water,
make love in the air
nestled under water,
surface the clouds
in the no-other-word-for-it blue.
Who says the sun doesn't swim
in the mountains of the moon?
This is a jungle of a garden,
and I'd rather die with your orchid
in my mouth
than live forever talking weather
with the weeds.

Do you hear me?
I would rather die
with your orchid
in my mouth
than live forever
talking weather
with the weeds.

Sea Glass

for Margaret

Hunched over
      like an egret,
my sister, Margaret,
      rummages barefoot
through a shoreline
      sharp with shells.

She can spot
      a speck of sea glass
and snatch it
      from the backwash
faster than you can say
      mea culpa.

Shards that aren't
      soft, Margaret
tosses back into the froth,
      keeps only the worn,
frosted scraps of light,
      finished

fragments
      with a jagged past
thrashed around
      so long they've been
sanded down,
      finally,

rounded off,
      smoothed over,
dull, but translucent
      and elusive.
My sister
      has spent

half a century
      of summers bent
on a handful
      of cobalt blue,
a riptide ruby
      or two.

Swing Set

After the smoldering plastic poor box
wedged inside the radiator
triggered the fire alarm,

Mother Innocence made me scrape it free
from the blackened pipe with a ruler
because my desk was closest.

She told the class detention was the least
of the vandal's problems. He was going to burn
in hell forever but never be consumed.

I turned the melted poor box in my hand
and ran my finger along the slot
for charity.

Roger's bottom lip quivered.
Can't a sinner, said David, *go to confession
and then not get put in the fire?*

The head nun ruffled her gown and replied,
*He who confesses is forgiven
and enters heaven.*

What does he do there? David asked her.
Mother Innocence swelled up like a steeple bell
and tolled, *Those saved will see God's face.*

And then what? David pressed on,
turning his head toward the swing set
outside the window.

Then they will bask in His glory
and praise His name forever,
snapped the nun.

I saw David look from the swings
to the hillside blazing in maple leaves,
and I knew neither of us would admit to a thing.

Stoop Ball

My fingers and thumb
don't forget the squeaky
grip and hard rubber give
or the hours spent bouncing
a Pinky Ball off the front stoop.
My arm remembers the windup,
the spin, the snap of the wrist,
the release and release
until it got so I could stand
on my sidewalk, facing
the street, twirl and whip
the ball, spike the corner
edge of the front steps
and catch the rebound
behind my back.
I played alone, thaw
to frost, the bases
loaded. The traffic
held its breath. Maria
peeked from between
the curtains next door.
I threw my heart out
for years. How many pitches
is that? How many balls
and strikes? How many hits
given up, runs scored?
All of the losses
and perfect games
of the past don't add up
to anything.

It's always been about the ball
in hand and the man
at the plate, twisting
his cleats in the dirt,
cocking back the bat,
swinging with all he's got.

Stumbling Around in the Light

Something wasn't right.
I could tell by the way it wobbled
across the lawn, midafternoon.

Fat Head the cat knew it too
and kept back, pretending to lick a paw
each time the opossum stumbled.

When it collapsed, I stepped outside
as far as the side porch then stopped short
should it jump up rabid and bite me.

Maybe it just came for water,
a patch of clover, a pool of shade
to die in.

But what if the kids next door
corner it by accident?
There's a shovel nearby in the shed.

I could surprise it
in the back of the head,
but what with the body?

It could be harder to get rid of dead
than alive.
Wouldn't it be better to just let it be?

Maybe it isn't dying this time,
just sick and tired and stumbling
around in the light

looking for a place safe
or at least shaded
and as far away from pain as possible.

Maybe it isn't any more deadly
or closer to dying
than I am.

Poe Bernadette

Everyone remembers the beating
of the tattletale heart
beneath the floorboards,
but along with the terrors of Poe,
I keep a nun sealed up
in my mind. Sister Bernadette
reigned eighth grade with an eighteen-
inch ruler and two books,
one of which was Poe's complete works.

She knew his dark habits inside out
and taught us the tintinnabulation
of the word made flesh, then put to death
again and again, the blessed agony
and perpetual transubstantiation
scribed in language so sharp
that when she read to us, I could taste blood.

For four months, perched like a raven
in front of the class, Sister Bernadette
preached everything from *Genesis*
to *The Pit and the Pendulum.*
She slapped the rhythm of *The Bells*
on the blackboard with her ruler.
For four months she measured
what our memories lacked
with a smack across our open palms.
For four months we listened, read,
recited, and drilled. Four months
in perfunctory worship—
as in the very description
of hell that she gave us—
burning but not consumed.

Then, Sister Bernadette
was sent away. *On retreat,*
we were told. *Institutionalized,*
my father said. In my mind,
a padded cell, no bigger than the closet
in the back of the classroom
where her private lessons took place,
or the tight space under the floorboard
of my mouth where words,
bloodied and raw, were still beating.

Dear Sister Bernadette, for the instruction
that was excruciatingly passionate,
may you not be forsaken,
but like one of the thieves in the Bible,
given your own desk come the hereafter,
for you delivered unto me
not only the rote prose of discipline
and a trembling awe of authority,
but also the poetry of rebellion,
the dark tongue of God.

What I Wanted of Milkweed

I picked a milkweed pod from a field
and propped it in a vase on my desk
then made a game with students
of watching it shrivel dry, day by day,
and split open. While we trudged through
another novel, unlocked another plot,
a slit widened from the base of the casing
and spread to the tip of the husk.
It was the slowest opening any of us
had ever witnessed, the softest shedding.
Whenever anyone swept by or undid
a window anywhere in the classroom,
white hairs trembled inside, then peeled from
a gray pouch, and tumbled on the breeze.
I wanted to see who among the passing
between bells would notice wispy cocoons
bottled on a desk and not be able to resist
stopping in for a second, risk being late
for class, just to stroke the silk tufts
with a fingertip, maybe even pinch a seed
from a gray pod, dangle it in front of pursed lips,
whisper a wish, and blow it away with a kiss.
I wanted to know how long it would take
to fill the hallway with feathery white spheres
and an entire student body, distracted
by frayed bubbles bobbing around them,
turn away from their lockers and friends.
Caught up and spun by a sudden draft,
I wanted to watch students dip and weave,
careen off the walls on the way to physics
and history. What else is there to wish for
if not that a corridor of milky green tiles
and fluorescent lighting be quietly converted
into a swirling field of snow?

What knowledge is worth chasing after more
than that we can clasp in our hands?
How far have we come if we aren't struck downy
and transported by the world around us,
if we can't open our lives to what's sown
on the wind and drift into class late
but inseminated, or better yet, turn
at the first exit sign we find, burst
through the fire doors, and climb the sky?

Seaside Heights

This is the ocean before memory,
and those are the pelicans my grandfather
told me used to pilot the waves
before I was born.

I swear that's the same dolphin
that surfaces in my dreams,
and this is the sea glass my sister and I
gathered and polished like gems.

I understand what water means.
I have been thirsty all of my life.
Still, no matter how long it's been,
I've never forgotten how to swim.

I've seen the sea blue, gray, and green,
sharp as a bed of shells
and stellar with jelly fish.
And I've suffered its undertow.

So I take the sand very seriously,
and this year the beach grass
stitched in rows across the young dunes
is a promising binding.

But I know the waves, like pages
in the book of all there is to know,
turn over themselves as they come
and into their own as they go.

Timepiece

I began learning about sacred
and profane time when my silver,
stretch-band wristwatch stopped
at exactly twenty-six past nine
while I was horsing around
during my first communion,
according to my father,
whose watch was always right.

In black and white, young men
and women dove off stone coasts
into an exploding ocean without
damaging their Timexes on TV,
but the first and last watch
I ever owned was a gift ruined
right after it was given to me.

Whether the watch broke because
of something I did or not
doesn't matter now that my father's dead.
And I don't really recall
if it was nine twenty-six or half past ten.
Didn't ask for a watch to begin with.
I opened my mouth,
stuck out my tongue
and swallowed the timeless body of God.
But I don't remember that, either.
Only the grievance has outlived my father,
and it has nothing to do with censure
or setting things right
or why I haven't worn a watch since—
desperate as I am for any memory of him.

Peony

I used to bury my head like a mole
in the palm of my hand and tunnel
through book after book until one spring,
a woman opened the earth right outside
my front door with a single flower.
She said, *Touch a peony once*
and your head will shred into a thousand pages
just like mine. Just like mine, the ants
will peel the petals from your heart
every year for the rest of your life.
Then she offered me the peony,
and I touched it twice.

The Neighbor's Dog

If you fall asleep
to geese chortling
with the moon,
the neighbor's dog
will shame you
with its barking.

If you fall asleep
to rain playing
roof shingles
like black keys
on a grand piano
at the bottom of a lake,

the neighbor's dog
will shame you
with its barking.
If you can't sleep,
it's probably the barking.
No aria there.

Nor is the bark
staking a claim,
heralding a friend
or the moment.
It is by no means
a transcendent chant.

Eyes, teeth, and
cyclone fencing
glisten with rain
in yellow porch light.
Each accusation
snaps at the wind.

Judas

When I was twelve,
I learned enough Latin
to be an altar boy
and serve six a.m. Sunday mass.
It was always so quietly cold.
I thought the morning cracked open
when I rang the steeple bell
and unbolted the heavy oak door.

Dust swept from the radiators
toward the pews,
water turned into wine.
I suspended a gold plate
under a single file of yawns
as they rolled out their tongues
for a sliver of God.

I was a good altar boy.
I knew the stations of the cross by heart
and understood original sin was mine,
not mine to understand.
I accepted *spiritus sanctus*
translated as *holy ghost*
terrified children
and was better re-translated *holy spirit*.

I was a good altar boy,
even if sometimes I snuck a sip of wine
from the vestibule shelf,
took a little change from the collection box,
or, for a dollar, let the Father
put his tongue in my mouth.

A good altar boy.
Didn't I say no when he got on his knees
and offered me more money
to go further?
And when he threatened to tell my parents
I was stealing money from the poor
(he had known all along),
wasn't I good?
Who told them first,
told them everything?

Then why didn't they believe?
Why did my father drive me to the rectory
and make me accuse the priest to his face?
Why can't I remember anything
other than the way his black cassock
rose from behind the desk
and the dark echo in his voice
when he said, *I love all my children,*
somehow the boy has misunderstood.
Still, God forgives him
and all is forgotten?

He said, *All is forgotten.*
That part was right.
I saw my mother forget
even as I told her.
And my father?
I can't remember now what he said,
only what I didn't hear.

The Only Symphony

Who isn't drifting inside and out
at the same time? Whose heart doesn't float
like a paper-thin note on the wind?

I have been watching the leaves
do their annual leaving, watching the wind
scoop over and under them, twisting
this way and that and back again
until they turn into the ground.
And I have been turning myself.
Do you know what I mean?

Have you ever considered your life's like an elevator,
always departing as well as arriving, each floor
another ceiling; every ceiling, a floor?

But I drift, don't I?
I was talking about the leaves,
the way they swirl as they fall.
I was dipping and rising
like a rabbi davening,
rocking to the left, to the right,
the way some leaves cradle the air,
like gentle pendulums, swaying
back and forth like children
riding swings, like brooms
sweeping away what's right
and what's left in one motion,
like the ebb and flow of the ocean,
or the hands of the maestro inside us
conducting the only symphony we know.

The Original Tree

It isn't until noon the fog lifts.
First, a red maple burns through
the mist, then an orange burst
of trees. I was afraid rain
would steal fire from the leaves,
but now the forest is ablaze,
and I stroll with a daughter
swinging from each of my hands
like splashing buckets of water
down a trail of ashes
into flickering woods.
I tell the girls that warm days
and cold nights sweeten trees,
give color to their leaves,
but as winter presses in,
they grow tired and spread
a patchwork quilt over their roots
to keep them snug until spring.
My older daughter doesn't believe me
and turns back a slab of leaves
in the path with her foot.
She says the underside is slimy,
black, and sour as a swamp.
Her sister wants to know
if trees dream when they sleep.
The forest shuffles into a field.
A whirlwind of leaves struggles
like a desperate tornado
to piece together the original tree.

The Way of the Cage

I couldn't take the gnawing, the hint
of urine under the floorboards. I worried
about wires, lights chewed out,
or finding a nestling mummified
if I tried poison in the eaves, so I
Have-a-Hearted, plastered peanut butter
to trigger plate and waited. Caught six
squirrels in two days. The last two at once.
Transported the first one by car trunk
across state lines to a park on the other side
of the river climbing in oak trees.
But when I returned with the second,
a young one with a nicked ear, there were
too many rangers. As I was leaving,
a blue arrow pointed south, the sign read
New Life Island, and I thought, how fitting,
but when I arrived, the gate was padlocked.
So I apologized to the second squirrel
and opened the cage door
in the driveway to the Kingdom Hall.
Let go the next four in the same place.
I like to think of them bedded down together
in a nest padded with shredded pamphlets,
up to their haunches in Watchtowers,
or praying to acorns in their devout paws
as if eating apples with both hands.
I do not believe squirrels are beneath
or beyond conversion, but I doubt to convert me
they will zigzag upstream, the way they do
in the street, too fast to sink. However,
there *is* a bridge. And this morning

I watched a small squirrel with a nicked ear
tightrope telephone wires from my house
to the church across the street; saw it again,
digging sporadic holes in my yard.
And though I suspect someone from the other side
is shipping squirrels back across the river
to my street, I have no proof. And I am afraid
of what it is inside me that wishes I owned a gun.
I know I shouldn't blame the squirrel
for wanting what it buried for safekeeping
before I drove it out of town,
but I can't take the gnawing,
the hint of urine under the floorboards.
I worry about wires, lights chewed out.

Alpha

I come for the stubble,
for the honey brown
and blackened rows
of corn stalks stitched
in strips of snow and
dried grasses, wind-
rattled free of all but
the most stubborn seed.

I come for the Rough-
legged Hawks that rode
nor'easters down from
the Arctic, come to see
their feathered strength
and patient talons hover
above shivering fields.

I want to witness the
persistence of harriers
swooping in low, back
and forth between rows,
for mice and voles
hunger-driven
from snug burrows.

I come to give thanks
for my ease and comfort,
and ask forgiveness
for having taken too little
care of these, the Horned Larks
and Snow Buntings
pecking seed cast
on asphalt at my feet,
the distant cows
huddled, steaming
in ice-glazed terrain.

I come to apologize
for my trespasses
and pay homage,
standing silent
in the salted cinders,
listening to swirls
of Snow Geese bark
like an angelic choir
of seals, my eyes fixed
on wing tips dipped
in black ink
and what they write
on beams of light between
the cloud-smudged sky
and white fields
drifting over
Oberly Road.

The Book

in memory of Ruth Twichell Cochrane

My friend Ruth
was writing a book
that traced the origin
of a small boat
and an altar stone
and possibly a man
connected with both
who refused to carry a gun
and first set foot
in the new world
with a hoe in his hands
so that the natives
would know him
to work with the land.

Our last visit
I brought biscotti,
and Ruth put up tea
and told me while
researching the boat,
she overturned a lead
about the stone
in an obscure sentence
in an equally obscure book.
Then she said the doctor
told her there was little
writing time left.

I asked what would happen
if she didn't finish,
and she put her hand
in mine on the table,
leaned close, and said,
There isn't any boat.
I made up the bit
about the altar stone,
and, as for the man
with the hoe in his hands,
he was really my great-
great-grandmother.
And the hoe was a book.

What Are the Odds of Moonlight?

for Catherine

Some people believe the moon is the night's eye
or the sun's sister or a mirror
in which to see themselves wax and wane.
They want to know each of its craters
by name.

How the moon lifts and lets fall oceans
or winks in slow motion are fields of study
for someone other than me.
That it paves a white road across dark water
is the talk of poets.

What I love most is the way moonlight
pools in the small of her back
as she crouches on the dock
and leans over the lake to unfasten
the rowboat.

Autumn Song

A leaf scuffs
              its brown shoe
across the street
              like a record needle
skipping
              through an old song
reminding me
              I have not heard
my father sing
              or say a single thing,
not even in
              the muffled branches
of my dreams,
              for over twenty years.
I don't forget
              the songs he taught me
but I would trade them all,
              without a doubt,
to hear the voice
              that bore the words
like wings
              as they flew
from his mouth.

Winter Birds

I am more at home
with the clucks and clickings
of winter birds
than the warbling melodies of spring,
more at ease
with the hack-tapping of woodpeckers
riddling trees with their drilling.

I like my forests brittle
and scrambling with squirrels.
There's something sincere
about White-throated Sparrows,
something honest among crows.
What more does a junco need
than an empty pocket of snow
and a couple of ragweed seeds?

Friends say winter's drab
and frozen-shut tight.
They swear I'm obsessed
with a desperate knocking,
but I want to know what the owl
asks of the night.
I want to read the stars
like a hawk
in broad daylight.

Bright Green Hose, Early Sixties

We were at war back home, too.
If it wasn't with the Vietnamese on TV,
then it was against the suburban outdoors.
I was always in training. My father, a lieutenant
in the reserves, would order me to look on
as he stopped short a mole tunneling
through his trim lawn by driving a pick ax
into the head of the miniature mountain range
buckling up across the yard. Once, I stood
at attention humming taps while he wrapped
an old tee shirt around a stake, soaked it
in kerosene, and torched a tent caterpillar nest
in a birch tree. The dark-bellied web burst
into flames like the *Hindenburg*, hundreds
of charred larvae rained on the sidewalk.
I rubbed the last of them out like burnt wicks,
hash-marked the white cement with their tally,
then clothes-pinned baseball cards to my bike
so they'd flap in the spokes motorcycle-loud
when I zigzagged through clouds
sprayed from the back of the mosquito truck.
I pretended I was piloting a fighter plane
firing at the oncoming Vietnamese,
while my father doused the smoldering tree
with a bright green hose from Sears.

Local Holy Wars

The old woman who feeds squirrels walnuts
doesn't care what a plague her charity is
on the neighborhood. Her kindness,
like rocks, has to be hand-picked or troweled
from every flower bed and vegetable garden in town.
A man on Third Street can't sleep
for the pirating of tiny feet across his ceiling.
Twice so far this fall he has shoveled
a treasure trove of shells piled high in his attic
into the trash and secured his eaves with chicken wire.

Still there's no talking sense to the old woman
who never had children of her own to feed
and rattles inside her house like a gourd
full of dried-up seeds. She believes she's a saint,
St. Francine of Frenchtown. Her neighbors
say she's nuts. Call her Sister Squirrelly.
But she swears they're all pagans
who should celebrate, not crucify, squirrels,
and she hurls a litany of curses after them
as they zigzag through the backyards and alley ways
behind Brother Tom of the BB gun.

We Now Know

We now know stars are holes in the night
into which fishermen toss their dreams
for the great whale.

We also realize such an immense creature
will not fit through a drop of light.

Some of us must remain behind and polish the lakes
while others learn to hold their breath
and swim through the darkness forever.

Lived Like a Saint

One summer I lived like a saint.
I didn't work, learned thrush,
and walked barefoot among bees.
I left a moth tugging at a web
for the spider
and split my garden with the weeds.

Crows barked in hickories.
They could have been clarinets;
it was all music to me.
They played a song about compost,
perched on a gray and shaggy limb
and waited for my bread.

Part cicada, part katydid, heartbeat
and drone, days plodded by
or whirred like hummingbirds,
a trace of basil in the wake of their wings.
I couldn't tell stars from fireflies.
I heard lunaria sing.

in the flock of geese
escher did not draw
each bird is a part
of the profile
of a larger bird
that shifts shape
as it unwinds
along the horizon
like a ribbon
a wedge driven
into the setting sun
the last three birds
a series of periods
trailing a sentence
an aerial ellipsis
something left unsaid
to be continued
in the blueprint of a sky
more sublime
than ever even escher
had in mind

The Rabbit

Sometimes I think the whole world's
propped up on paws
like the rabbit I passed in the street,
arched from stomach to head
as if it were trying to push up from the road,
keep from being pulled in,
shifting side to side
unable to lift the mangled legs
dragging behind it.

I think how it held back its shoulders
while I made a U-turn, how quietly it shook
when I pulled up alongside it,
how a black sports car stopped too
and the guy riding shotgun without a shirt on
poked his head through the sunroof and said,
We were gonna put it outta misery.

So was I, I said, *Go ahead.*

But, before I could pull away he asked,
Would you do it?

I don't want to talk about brittle mercy,
the soft inside of a skull,
how fur slides on asphalt,
or about how less than fifteen minutes later,
as I was driving back home from the store,
a Turkey Vulture shrugged
on what was left of the carcass.
I can still see the black feathers
shrouding its throat,
the red face, the white tip of its beak.

The next day the rabbit was gone,
and I ran into one of the same guys
renting videos. But the tongue is harder to lift
than both legs, so we didn't say a thing
about remorse or the undriveable distance
between compassion and slaughter,
didn't even offer a handshake,
just a faint smile, something quick with the eyes.

I want to talk about what a waste it is
not to say what needs to be said
while the words are still in the mouth,
because nothing lives on the tip of the tongue
forever. I want to know what silence
has to do with survival and why we live
with all the things we don't say,
all the muted stains that darken the road.

Echo Lake

to my left, cold
December sunrise
at my back. Driving
home from Maxwell House,
Hoboken, New Jersey,
after eight hours steeping
up to my knees
in fifteen-foot
coffee vats,
high-pressure-
water-cleaning
oily-bean residue
from stainless-steel walls.
The graveyard shift
behind me. Highway
ahead, Echo Lake
to my left. In low
swoops a Canada Goose,
skims the roof
of the blue Buick
in front of me,
plunges toward my hood,
banks on a rush of air.
I have one hand
on the wheel,
the other dialing
in the radio. When I look
to the rear-view mirror,
white feathers
explode from the grill
of a bread truck
behind me.

The DJ
announces,
Late last night
John Lennon
was shot dead,
and sunlight
strikes the ice-
glazed lake
like a match.

Dylan's Pool Cue

I played the eight off the fifteen
and stumbled back in time
to the day after Christmas, 1969,
when I sank Maria in the corner pocket
of the street in front of her house,
neighbors outside shoveling snow.
Then I banked two summers later in the side
and knocked on her door, rum-and-Coked
and smoking a Camel to cover the smell
as I asked for the gift back,
the pool cue she gave me,
the one I'd left behind in my hurry
while she was finger-picking "Don't
Think Twice," and I stormed out insisting
I was sick and tired of *Dark Shadows*
and the *Enquirer*, rather than chalk up the truth,
that I'd started a new rack without her.
I remember she dropped her guitar,
and chased after me into the road,
but I shoved her aside,
right in front of her neighbors.
I still see her collapsed
like a bare spot in the white-felted street.
But by 1971, I was reigning king
of the Idle Hour pool table
and decreed I deserved my own stick.
Maria grimaced, at first,
then looked relieved
as she handed me the cue
without saying a word.
It's alright, I told myself. She was
alright. Don't think twice.

The Calling

At what sounds like a squadron
of seals or a thousand dogs barking overhead
and getting louder, I stop stirring the sauce
and run to the porch.

Sure enough, up above the house,
flocks of geese wedged together look to roost
along the river.

Their cryptic runes and raucous
honking, like clockwork, announce dawn and dusk
all winter long.

I watch them divide the sky
with aerodynamic government, and I feel afeather
with the couple that flock together for life
as well as the lone bird veering off
on a breeze of its own.

The father in me nods and throws
back his shoulders because I have seen the goose
hiss, snap and charge, without self-regard,
wings slapping at anything threatening
its fuzzy goslings.

When a floppy one, lagging behind,
flaps by, I want to catch it up with the others.

I want to join them myself,
as they descend the late light like gods
and ski on the water.

Lilacs

for Catherine

After the words swim
        from my mouth
and the letters of her name
        scatter
like minnows
        in the tributaries
of the wind,
        my last thought
will be lilac.

When not even
        the memory
of her memory
        remains,
my last thought
        will be lilac
and linger in
        the white forest
of her hair.

Towpath

I took the towpath upstream,
past the last homes on 12th Street, past
the cyclone fence fencing in rusty oil drums
stacked outside the abandoned factory,
past a poison ivy vine wrapped
around a sycamore tree like a hairy python
squeezing bark from the trunk, shed scales
teetering in the breeze on the cinder trail.
Erosion-exposed roots dipped
from the bank into the current and trapped sticks,
plastic bottles, cans, balls and bald tires
riding the river down from towns north.
Up ahead, oily orange sludge leached
from the weed-stubbled mound of clean fill
bulldozed over the Superfund site and oozed
through the woods into the river.
I got off before the stench,
stepped from the leafy green cloak of Virginia creeper
and wild grape draping the forest edge,
and climbed the hill behind Tom's Garage.
To my left, in a field of chicory
and thistle between the river and the road,
I saw what Monet saw in the wind and made
of light, a pink and blue cathedral.

Bird Call

Because spring rolls away winter's stone
and daylight pushes back the night.

Because of Black-throated Blue Warblers
and red trillium to come.

Because the Osprey on the power lines
by the river flies from its stack of sticks
but always comes back.

Because it circles above me,
perched on a clump of dead grass,
a tiny island in the oily mud.

Because I am surrounded
by discarded bones of shad
plucked midstream on their way home.

Because I do my best Fish Hawk,
which is the worst song that bird has heard
since I sang for it last fall.

Because the power tower,
like a giant cheese grater,
shreds the wind.

Because fresh red buds blister
on green stems.

Because the river scales its banks,
bursts open, spreads
a fertile layer of silt

over skunk cabbage
leafing fetid from its spathe
when the Osprey answers my call.

Snow Goose

The Snow Goose facing
the north wind upstream,
but being blown south,
its back to what lies ahead,
reminded me of the angel
of history Walter Benjamin
saw in a painting of Paul Klee's,
aching to change the catastrophe
piling up behind it,
but being sucked backwards,
unwillingly, into tomorrow,
and what has become
of the Susquehanna River,
what we have done to it,
the filth we have filled it with
we call progress.
But for all I know,
the Snow Goose
peers into north wind
for a lost mate
or the white nest
beyond the timberline
of its youth. For all I know,
the goose is a goddess
that splits currents in half
with her feathery wedge
or weaves them in and out
of each other.
She might be the mother
of all nursery rhymes, at that,
listening to wind
skip on water
for her next line.

Or just another fatty meal
for the plucking.
I could spend my life
guessing at everything
I don't know, making deities
of what's right in front
of me, but instead, I am facing
the coming year head on,
budging my wings
against the wind,
thrusting them open,
lifting myself up from alongside
that backwards bird
and pressing forward
into the frigid but clear
blue air.

What One of My Thoughts Thought
When It Thought I Wasn't Paying Attention

I should bust out of these cells,
pass like a ghost
through the thick wall of his skull
or lower myself in a tear
down one of his cheeks,
then drip from his chin to freedom,
leave him lost in the moment,
immediately primitive.

I want to occur
to something else.
Let a bottle cap have an idea for a change
or a shoe. Be the first thing to pop
into a groundhog's head.
I am sick of *his* theories.
I have a few of my own:
He isn't, I am. He's just putty in my hands.

His body is what I slip into
when I want to eat pizza,
listen to rain fall, fuck, or sing,
but flesh is a sensitive outfit.
In a single generation,
it wears thin.

I have to laugh when he points to his head
and says his insights come like lightning.
If he only knew how long it takes
for me to sink in. But some things
are best kept to myself.
He thinks he carries me within
like a candle in a dark cave
or a light bulb he flicks off and on at whim.
He makes science and religion
out of shadows I cast on the inside of his skull.

If he had even the slightest notion
I am just passing through—in one ear,
out the other—he'd be beside himself.
He couldn't handle the thought
that he's no more than a sponge
on the bottom of my ocean.
He credits his appetite for progress
with keeping his species alive,
but I've swallowed whole civilizations
of his kind to survive.
Where does he think he got the idea
he's at the head of the food chain, anyway?

Turning Over the Earth

I turned over the earth
and sowed a necklace of peas
beneath the worm-riddled moon
on Saint Patrick's Day again,
even though I know the ritual's contrived,
and I will be distracted by the ocean,
my tidy rows neglected and overgrown
come summer's end. But it's spring,
and when forsythia opens its yellow eyes
and shakes its head in the wind
like a sleepy sun, I am eager
for a plot to tend, my own garden,
soil that smells not of Mesopotamia
or a clover-covered bank in Ireland,
but of Delaware River bed, here
on Third Street, where I never tire
of the sleight of hand that planting is:
how seed vanishes into a hole in the ground
then reappears dancing the salsa
inside a jalapeño pepper; here,
where summer breezes through the garden
stirring tomatoes and basil into an aria
about a cloven heart of garlic,
and the sweet corn is all ears.
I have a recipe for hot cherry peppers
stuffed with garlic, onions, and anchovies
then fried until the bottoms blacken
that will make you cry for crusty bread
to sop up the oily residue on your plate.

For those peppers alone,
I will turn over the garden as long as I can,
and because I need to keep close to the earth,
feed my loved ones of my own hand,
feed the compost what we don't eat,
sow myself in time with those before me,
join the harvest.

I Didn't Go

for Catherine

I didn't go to Italy,
not a foot inside the big boot,
didn't tour the pagan capital
or the home of the stone-
made man,

nor the city made stone
and buried in ash, either,
or the city sinking
into the sea.

I roamed this rim
of the ocean,
stayed close
to my source.

I am a river
that would be a spring,
a droplet
of underground rain.

But my love
is a fountain
of wind.

Dreaming in Pompeii

He was dreaming of her in Pompeii,
his head, a stony egg,
nestled in her lap,
the porous pumice of her hand
at rest on the gray ash of his face.

Time cooled lava into solidified foam.
Their bones, a petrified city.
Two hearts' ruins entombed.
The entire civilization of their love
buried for centuries
beneath the sleep of stone.
Her hand caressing his cheek.

His head, nestled in her lap,
unearthed, but not awakened,
oblivious to whatever
archeologists or tourists—
not to mention poets—
might make of them
or of her hand
at rest on his face,
the way a bird settles on its egg,
waiting for him to awaken
and fly with her
far from the petrified ruins
of Pompeii.

A Case of Unopened Boxes

The Marquis of Debris returned from the Riviera
just in time for New Year's at Jane's studio,
a lofty A-frame with framed nudes reclining on the walls.

Jane hired the Good Kissers for the party:
a local lawyer on guitar and the guy from Wooden Nickel
spitting into a harmonica between vocals
while Lucky plucked bass like a bullfrog.

The crowd flexed the floor like a trampoline,
sheetrock bulged; heavy dancing mixed with wine
and bourbon and served in a room full of smoke
was bound to explode. The Marquis broke
for the door; outside the river swam in moonlight.
Leaning against the porch railing, he struck up a deal
to dispose of boxes—no questions asked—for a stranger.

Poised on the top step, Eric the Artist,
wearing a scarf like a noose and holding a cigarette
as if he were offering his head on a platter,
recited his aesthetic theory to the stars.
I want to paint everything, everything.

The Marquis said, *You can start with my balls.*
Max didn't laugh; he was the stranger.
He bought the boxes without looking inside,
and he needed to get rid of them quick
because he couldn't keep from peeking much longer.

The door to Jane's studio flapped like a hand
muffling a mouth stretched wide with song
and screaming every time someone opened it.

Tiny Moon

I spy a tiny moon
slip through a tear in the sky
and hang from a blue tree
in a field along the river.
I spy a cloud of Snow Geese
lift the blackened tips
of a thousand wings
from a winter corn field
and flag the wind
a single message.
A Red-tailed Hawk ousts a vulture
from a deer carcass
frozen roadside, rips
frosted skin from ribcage
even as I drive by.
I spy a snowflake sway in slow
motion to a clarinet solo
only the river can hear,
spy sheets of ice slide by
like continents adrift,
spy crow bury gold kernel
in bone labyrinth.
Patience, green lips!
I spy a tiny moon—
for some child other than I to spy—
slip through a tear in the sky
and hang from a blue tree.

Way-back Seat

for my mother

I don't remember if the moon was out or not,
but we drove up and down the night,
and after the Edison Memorial Bridge,
the Perth Amboy drive-in beamed by
with James Bond dodging Odd Job's
razor sharp bowler hat zipping at him
like a deadly Frisbee
while I sat in the way-back seat,
the one facing the rear-view window
of my mother's green station wagon.

I watched the movie screen shrink
like a sugar cube of light
and dissolve in an inky sky
until it blinked off around a bend.
A caravan of white eyes trailed behind us
and tail lights shot north like red stars.

Smooth blue sea glass
I snatched from the undertow the summer before
rubbed inside my lucky pocket
and thoughts of what the shore
might have in store in the morning
kept me awake
until the road humming lulled me under.

Sometimes, when I feel old and alone,
I go back to the way-back seat,
my mother's watery spirit behind the wheel,
father's solitary ghost at home gardening,
my weary sisters leaning like dominoes
on our generous brother
caught in the backwash that memory is.
I try to salvage them as they were,
hold fast a handful of gems.
I try to piece us together again,
reassemble the past washed overboard,
dashed to the sea.

For fifty years, I have combed Jersey beaches,
keeping an eye out and a hand ready
to grab a glimmer of sea glass
from the tumble of shells.
I have filled mantels of vases
with their smooth petals.
So far, my prize is a cloudy chip of red,
edges softened, frosted, worn so amorphous
by ocean and sand—not to mention the wear
of my own hands—that I can only imagine
how the jagged break first felt.

My Grandfather's Game

I spent a good part of any visit
in my aunt's basement studying
my grandfather's game: how he
picked a pool stick from the rack,
held the thick end in his right hand
and waved the tip up and down
to gauge the weight, then rolled it
on the table to check the level.
I watched him chalk up like
he was sharpening a giant pencil
and blow the loose blue dust off
when he finished. And I leaned in,
as he leaned low over the table
to get a cue-ball view, and mimicked
the pedestal of his left hand perched
like a bird on the felt lawn, his definitive
stroke. My grandfather believed
gentlemen called every ball, each kiss
and cushion, with just a tilt of the stick
or a nod in the pocket's direction.
He claimed my uncle's bridge
and short cue were cheating.
He would rather prop himself on one foot
and stretch across the table
or twist the stick behind his back
and bend his body around the beam
by the side pocket to make a shot.
Grandpa didn't play my father's game, either,
no triple combinations or double banks.

He always left easier shots for himself
to make. He taught me the geometry
and gesture of pool, and nine points
of English. *It's all about the leave*, he said.
He'd wave a finger when I bent to shoot:
Keep an eye out for the scratch,
then poke me in the ribs and chuckle,
and don't choke on the eight.

The Rewarded

What if the more at peace the spirit is
the more violently the body dies?
Ultimate pain is a saint going up in flames.
The flesh bubbles, peels back
from the bones of the good,
like red pages torn from a sacred text
which has never been understood.
One that proclaims
only the cold-blooded
are among those who die in their sleep, smiling,
while the humble, the kind,
those compassionate their entire lives,
suffer beyond any suffering
they'd ever had in mind.
And all of this not,
as you might expect,
because God has a twisted reward
in store for us,
but in order that the pure of heart
might pass through the vile side
of the world they leave behind
so that there will be nothing
they want to remember,
nothing they would bring with them,
not so much as a single strand of hair,
when the rapture claps
and they vanish forever
into the blessed, happy air.

this poem is called without frames because i was thinking about
how my father never framed his paintings he said his work was a
part of the wall and the room it was in as well as what was on the
canvas which reminded me of the time he volunteered to restore
the oil painting of st. vincent de paul above the altar of the
church we belonged to even though he wasn't catholic he brought
three loaves of bread and me to church one saturday morning
and starting at the top of the saint's head we polished the halo
then rubbed his face clean with the slices they shredded and fell
in crumbs at the foot of the ladder like the snow in the only
painting of my father's i own it's an abstract of the great swamp
in winter blue-gray tree trunks bulge from black ice with snow
skirts spread out around them the painting looks more like a
microscopic view of nerves with white dendrites my father was
trying to get at the fact that the swamp we went walking in was
also inside us i even remember the bend in the trail we were
walking on when the idea first came to him just as I recall the
way his small hands massaged the saint's face with the slices of
bread wiping away the dust soaking up the grime without leaving
a scratch i quit the church long before they tore it down for
something modern and new two-car-garage homes with exotic
landscaping edged in on the swamp for years before my father
died we buried his ashes at the foot of his favorite tree now all
I have is his painting and what lives without frames between lives

Into the Glare

Right now, I'm Ray Ban, the man
behind the brand I'm wearing,
more of a Wayfarer than those Aviators
like Kennedy or Monroe who flew
too close to the sun. Still,
light-weight ergonomics
help bear the brunt
of my tinted world view.

I'm Ray, the guy on checkout line
sporting his shades indoors
like Roy Orbison who remembers
the apple juice he forgot
he came for because
he was daydreaming about
Kim Novak wearing nothing
but Wayfarers on the Cote
d'Azur —or was it Gloria
Steinem and General MacArthur
arm wrestling naked? Anyway,

this Ray works his way through a line
of disgruntled shoppers
rattling their carts like cages,
snatches a bottle of apple juice
from aisle nine, and makes it back
in time, grinning like John Belushi
singing *with my hair slicked back*
and my Wayfarers on
before the cashier finishes
ringing up his order.
You know what I'm saying?
I'm more of your average spectacle,
just a modest display.

I picked a scratched and cloudy pair
of dollar-store sunglasses
from a pocket of ocean
and hid happily behind them
for seven days until broken,
only to be delivered by surf
the same day a brand new pair
of Ray-Bans, concealment
and celebrity hinged with erotic,
iconoclastic allure.

Now I'm no Andy Warhol
or Ray Stegeman, either,
just a guy doing his time,
nor is my identity framed
or confined by a product line
Tom Cruise revived with *Risky Business*,
but you know what I'm saying:
if a wave hands me Ray-Bans,
I wear them; if not,
I squint and keep staring.

Bonfire

I don't know about this fall; everything's burning.
I don't think I'll survive.
Everywhere I go the trees are on fire.
I try to hide, but I'm drawn to the flames.

I don't know about the sky either.
I've never seen such a steel-hard blue
nor felt a chill as disturbing as this before.

The leaves tremble from the trees,
and I feel my hands shaking.
The wind tosses them around;
my thoughts swirl up, then ground.
I can't take breaking away anymore.

I think the Osprey I saw sweeping yesterday's dusk
was the saddest of passings.
Last summer, together, we watched them
fold back their wings and plunge
under the ocean waves.

The silver fish they surfaced with were all they needed,
but when I look at the sky left in their wake,
I am filled with an empty space.

I don't know about her eyes.
I don't think I can take them turning away
anymore than I can put out the burning inside me
or rake in the flames. Everywhere I go
the trees are on fire. I try to hide,
but I'm drawn to the flames.

Market Street

Whether it was his receding silver hair slicked back
and trimmed tight or the waxed tips of his moustache
I noticed first when he turned his head our way,
I knew without looking his shoulders were upright,
and I wasn't surprised wing-tipped shoes matched
his white leisure suit or that they clicked off each step
along the sidewalk with purpose. I knew he wore cufflinks,
though I couldn't see his sleeves. And a tie clasp.
The pin kind, I bet. And he was all about his watch.
Though I couldn't see that either. But I have been studying
men all of my life. He winked at me and nodded slowly
at my wife as he passed by us on her side then hurled
a sharp glance at the hunched woman three steps back
in a brown housedress, her sweaty red face twisted in pain
as she hobbled after him fast as she could, muttering something
I didn't understand. And I wasn't sure how much her hurt
was physical—something in a leg or the hips—or how much
it was something else, or if she was pleading or pissed off,
but I knew he knew. Yet, for two blocks, he didn't ease up
or even nod in her direction. After the second intersection,
he paused at a shoe-store window display, leaned forward
and touched the glass at the red high heels just as she caught up
with him. Then he stood fast, and without looking at any of us,
turned and strode on, a bit slower—but not much—with her
quietly wincing along at his side. I reached over for my wife's hand,
slipped my fingers between hers and squeezed. She looked at me,
wary, but pleased. I wanted to stop right there and apologize,
but I didn't know what for. Apparently, she did, and squeezed back,
though this time her eyes lowered a bit, turned inward,
and we both held tight and made a left at Mulberry.

Primal Urge

While waiting with my daughter
in the waiting room of Primal Urge Piercing Salon,
I thumbed through a photo album
of satisfied clientele: eye-hooked
and belly-button-studded teenagers
with tiny batons puncturing their tongues,
a pregnant woman in nipple rings, old men
with everything from ears to testicles rung.

A girl standing nearby, who looked
like she gave blood for a living, asked the friend
whose back she was using to write on
right out loud, *Did you tell the truth on number nine?*
Her friend rolled her eyes at the rest of us,
threw up her hands, and snapped back at her,
They won't do it if we tell 'em we're high, stupid,
and then they fell over each other laughing.
I whispered to my daughter, *We can still leave.*
She glared at me and shook her head.

After I signed the release form,
the doctor of piercing appeared
wearing a white lab coat and a black tie.
My daughter, her skin as pale as the moon
on the night she was born, whispered to me
she was scared, squeezed my hand, then stood quickly
and followed him down the hallway into a room,
while I sat in the waiting room waiting,
something sharp running through me.

Tending the Garden

Your goal was perennial, maintenance-free,
something always in bloom, the palette ranging
three seasons: ecstatic daffodils to rusty
chrysanthemums, well-mulched and drip-
irrigated—you bent and clamped the hose
back on itself, hammered nail holes the length,
snaked it through rock beds. But honestly,
flowers never meant much more than pretty to her.
She learned a few names, but could always
just ask. I watched her from the kitchen window
the day after the service on her hands and knees
swatting at the halo of gnats swarming her head,
pulling up weeds, crying, cursing your name.

The Great Swamp

As kids we skinny dipped
in the Passaic River off of
White Bridge Road where
the water made a clean break
from the Great Swamp
and headed south.

Swinging out over the stream,
we let go the rope and parted water,
plunged our toes deep
in the leechy mud, then sprang
back and broke surface with
a scream.

We took turns at the rusty wheel
of an abandoned Chevy
imprisoned by birch trees
and told bloody stories
of young lovers parked
in the murky dark.

We believed in campfire guitar,
our smoky voices rising
like tributaries
into the fathomless night.

But even as we sang,
the river was dying.
National Gypsum
dumped asbestos
into the water downstream,
the first of many things
we weren't aware of
on the way to the ocean.

Shroud of Frenchtown

I made the Shroud of Frenchtown
after I finished sanding the stairwell
in my house, pressed the print
of my face into a sweaty t-shirt,
and left a spackle-dust ghost
in the damp navy blue cloth
then hung it to dry in my basement.
    That night I dreamt a century
swung by like a wrecking ball
and beat the house to rubble,
but in the ruins, an archeologist
found my shroud, and from the sweat
and dust of my features approximated
my race, age, height, weight, political
affiliation, religion, and shoe size.
    But what he didn't know
was that I patched, puttied, and sanded
the stairwell myself. The archeologist
had no clue that blasting iTunes,
I sang along with Arcade Fire,
and our anthem blazed up the staircase,
swept down the hall and leapt from the attic
to the quiet house next door.
    When I woke, I drew a fine line
with a brush between primed wall and
white ceiling then danced as I rolled on
both coats of bright yellow. Finished,
the stairwell beamed like a tunnel
through the sun, and I climbed the steps
and descended them proudly wrapped
in what I'd done.

Retired Anarchist

It took a while to get used to having nothing to do,
to stop keeping track of the time, until the days
no longer gathered like fleas but began to drift
like hot air balloons, unnumbered and nameless.

Finally, I gave in to the humidity, fell behind
with the weeding, and turned over my garden
to the thistle and morning glories. Now, I hammock
like a turtle on his back in the green shell
of my yard and read Socrates or go swimming.

I like to think I'm still one of the gnats
and that I would draw blood, or at least gnaw
on the ear of injustice. But what does it matter?
It's almost autumn. Why compete with the wasps
and their perfect architecture of paper?
Why not relax and let each fall
come into its own season?

I can jackknife the water and swim
to the other side of the pool
or use what's left of my anger
to blow up a raft. I can sleep on the surface
beneath the fireflies and the stars.

My granddaughter is a splash in the water.
Soon she will sprout wings like her mother
and fly from my arid landscape for a fresh oasis.
Right now, she thinks I don't know
she's sneaking up on my float to tip it over.

Cicada

for Alanna

Even if we could live forever,
what if we still grew old and gray
as the dusk? What if we shrank
into the topsoil of the night
and woke whining for the sun
with voices so shrill and small
only termites could hear them?

I'd rather claw from the earth blindfolded
and drag my grimy shell up the side
of the whitest tree I can find,
rather scream like a match head on fire
than smolder and never die.
I would split open my spine
just to fly for one season.

I Got As Far As the Sycamore

I got as far as the sycamore,
rain-soaked and choking with grape vines.

A scar of poison ivy, thick
as a parade of tarantulas,
crept the length of a hollowed hickory nearby,

and an oriole I once knew as Baltimore
flashed past, orange as sunrise,
hooded and cloaked in night.

It was the morning after the sky split open,
turned inside out,
and forty years rained down.

I got as far as the sycamore.

Like blue pilot lights,
a pair of Indigo Buntings
ignited the underbrush.

Then, before me, the tree, bark blotched
and flaky, sloughing page
after silver-green page.

A Yellow-bellied Woodpecker
poked its head from a side door
in the nearby hickory.

I got as far as the sycamore,
then began my own shedding.

Into Sycamore

When I was young,
a crow coaxed me
into curling up inside
a gutted sycamore tree.
The air was ancient, cool.

Now sparrows perch on my limbs,
discuss the price of eggs
and tell dirty jokes
while swallows twitter
in my hollow.

I am a tangle of fibers
plugged into the earth,
exposed to light, grounded,
as ecstatic as the thunderbolt
that split me open.

It took a long time to learn
my heart wasn't a butcher block
but a hope chest, a trunk
swollen with memories.

Now, I tuck my seeds under my leaves,
work my roots like divining rods
into this evaporating star I call home,
and run my branches
through the mountains of the night.

Let my bark flake and fall away,
pile blotched landscapes at my feet.
What's it to me? I live for thirst.
The past is an empty cup.
There is water here.

Show of Teeth

for Genevieve

What is it about groundhogs
that can prod a good woman
to shoot one in her backyard
from her bedroom window
without even raising the screen?
I have run my finger
around the wire stubble
surrounding the hole,
and what I have seen
has touched me.

It all started when Genevieve
told me that both under-
and above-ground fencing
failed to keep a woodchuck
from shredding her lettuce,
and sampling—never eating—
an entire tomato. First,
she bought a Have-A-Heart trap,
but ended up relocating groundhogs
across river only to find fresh
groundhog deliveries
when she got home.
Then she bought the gun.

Shortly after, I met a trim-bearded man
in a coffee shop whose eyes lit up
when he told me that as a boy
he watched his father toss a match
down a burrow drenched
with kerosene. *Poof!*
he threw his hands in the air,
and fire jumped in his eyes.

After a poetry reading,
a woman in a red kerchief
poked me in the chest
with a pointed finger for emphasis
while swearing she had once swerved
her car toward a groundhog
sitting on its haunches
alongside the street:
Would've hit it
had it stayed put,
she screeched.

Then, last summer,
I found myself in the garden
poking a woodchuck with a hoe
until it clamped down on the blade
and wouldn't let go.
That's when I came face to face
with the cocky waddle
and stubborn show of teeth,
the tug-of-war that yanks us all
by the nape of our necks
and won't let us back down.
That's when I awakened
the beast with two names,
one that hibernates inside of me
like a primal secret, a shadow,
as dark as it is far from spring.

Remnants

If my father were alive and driving,
he would pull over
on the shoulder, brave traffic,
then thresh through the downcast
corn rows and crop the head
of the blackened sunflower
nodding among them.

He would twine it to an eyehook
in the basement beam to dry out
for future arrangements
alongside motherwort, milkweed,
snakeroot, carrion flower,
wormwood, heal-all, angelica,
and sweet everlasting.

My father rummaged all four seasons,
but there was something about fall
he had to gather and salvage,
something he needed to maintain.
He believed in the afterlife
of remnants and practiced
the art of arranging the remains.

Reservoir

for Abbie Hoffman

From the reservoir
a white island lifts,
tilts and takes flight
banking on swift
currents of air.
A tornado of Snow Geese
swirls in the blue sky
above the reservoir,
and the great body of water
turns with their circling,
churns counterclockwise,
time's black-and-white wings
shapeshifting. Arms
restored, fingers revived,
you pick a moment of winter
from a blue pocket
in the snow—a droplet, Abbie,
I know. But you steal life
back from the reservoir
to stand by my side,
if only for a cold breath
on the bank of being,
and watch Snow Geese rise
like an island of wings,
and we raise our fists
together in the frigid air.

The Gourd's Complaint

I was born to be useless
and sprawling,
not repulsively appealing,
to roll my heart out
like a carpet of leaves
guy-wired to the grass
then flower a white trumpet.
My inedible fruit intended
to swell from the vine
like a fat old sack of wine,
bitter and nauseating.

Make what you will of me,
maraca or birdhouse.
I'll rattle if you shake,
but I was meant to suckle
a creek from the soil
and devour platefuls of sun
for my seeds' preservation
alone. This shell
was supposed to be
biodegradable.

Now, thanks to you,
it's hand-painted
and lacquered
with a goofy blue face
and a red mouth
for Purple Martins
to dart in and out.
Thanks to you,
my hereafter
is a craft fair.

Babble

Where I live
blackbirds babble
in bamboo
fall through winter,
gather together
both ends of sleep,
and sing like a river
full of leaves.

Still, I have no reason
to think their song
is any more or less
than babble,
nor do I know
whether they are a choir
or a flock of solos.
I only know that we
should sound so good.

Shrew

I was born nervous.
When we were young,
at our father's command,
my sisters, brother, and I
locked teeth on one another's tail
and trailed behind him
trembling like a hairless caravan,
until I strayed off to the left,
slurred and erratic.

Now I am solitary and shrill
with a bit of Medusa in my bite.
I like my meals petrified
and divide my life
between earthworms and sleep.
Led by my nose,
I dig until I'm too tired to eat
then rest anywhere
I can lay my feet.

They say, of course, I am shrewd,
but that has thirteen meanings.
My heart rattles its hinges
when exposed to the wind.
I am burrowed in fear.
For five reasons alone, I survive.
Mine's a gnawing humility.
I eat as fast as I can,
hide poison inside me,
and keep a mean secret.

My Scribe

for Catherine

I don't know
that the stars
crossed our paths
anymore than I know
that they didn't.
But I *can* tell you
which birds
spelled her name
and the year of the fall
it was written
in the wind's
secondhand
calligraphy and signed
by autumn leaves,
as well as the river,
where each ripple
is a line of poetry
I cannot speak.
At best, I can say
I have seen her bow
over a box of light
illuminating letters
like a Blue Heron
studies the water for fish.
At best, I can say only
that the fish
the river delivered
like slivers of light
swam from the fingertips
of her hand.

Birder's Last Blessing

Leave the binoculars behind.
What good has bringing birds closer
brought them, anyway?

Let species spring
unidentified branch
to branch

and catapult
into the scrambled alphabet
of clouds.

Let wings alone
be sufficient, a glint of indigo,
dusk's fluted calling

spiraling to earth
like a handful of leaves,
the feathered thing before you.

May the names of all thirty-six warblers
—if you ever had them—
be the first to go.

May nothing fly from
the field guide of your mind
when iridescent emerald zipping

zips by a Kool-Aid-red feeder
hooked like bait
on the neighbor's gutter.

May you hover sipping nectar
from scarlet trumpets mid-flight
in nobody's garden.

John Smith lives in Frenchtown, NJ, with calligrapher Catherine Lent. He has three daughters.

John's poetry has appeared in numerous literary magazines and has also been anthologized in *Under a Gull's Wing: Poems and Photographs of the Jersey Shore* and *Liberty's Vigil: The Occupy Anthology*.

His poem, "Lived Like a Saint," which appeared in *The Journal of New Jersey Poets*, was set to music by Philadelphia composer, Tina Davidson, as part of a choral work, *Listening to the Earth*, commissioned by the New Jersey Parks Commission.

John's poetry has appeared in *NJ Audubon* since the late 1980s. His poem, "Birding," was commissioned by The New Jersey Audubon Society for its centennial.

CPSIA information can be obtained at www.ICGtesting.com
Printed in the USA
BVOW08s0415090813

327721BV00001B/26/P